The Muscular System

Katherine White

the rosen publishing group's
rosen
central

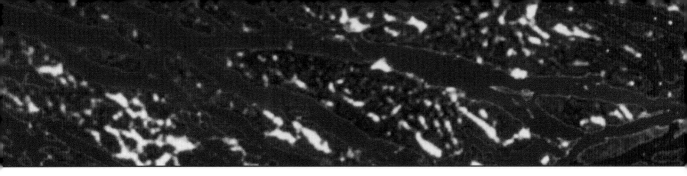

Published in 2001 by The Rosen Publishing Group, Inc.
29 East 21st Street, New York, NY 10010

First Edition

Library of Congress Cataloging-in-Publication Data

White, Katherine, 1975–
  The muscular system / by Katherine White. — 1st ed.
      p. cm. — (The insider's guide to the body)
  ISBN 0-8239-3340-7
  1. Muscles—Juvenile literature. [1. Muscular system. 2. Muscles.]
I. Title. II. Series.
  QP321 .W474 2000
  612.7'4—dc21
                                                        00-010382

Manufactured in the United States of America

Contents

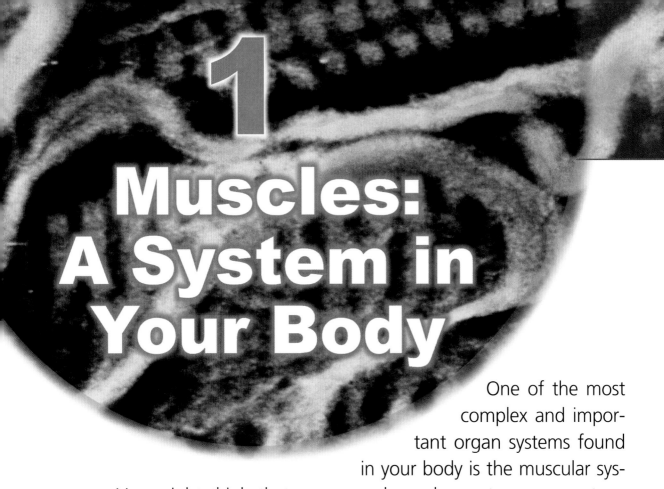

1
Muscles: A System in Your Body

One of the most complex and important organ systems found in your body is the muscular system. You might think that your muscles only create movement—a rather large task all by itself—but the muscular system does even more than that. Did you know that some of the muscles within your body are not under your control, or that one of the main types of muscle is found only in your heart? The muscular system is full of surprises.

However, before we venture off into the inner workings of the muscular system, you should know a bit about some of your other body systems because your muscles play a part in them, too.

The Circulatory System

The circulatory system is the system of your body that is made up of the heart; blood vessels (like your veins and arteries), which carry blood through your system; and capillaries, one-cell-thick blood vessels that connect tiny muscular fibers to the arteries and the veins. The blood vessels and muscles control the flow of blood throughout your body

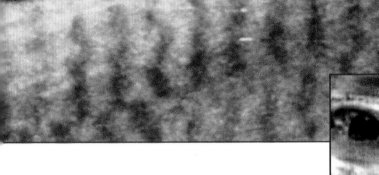

in a process called circulation. The circulatory system and the muscular system work together so that blood gets to the parts of your body that need it.

The Digestive System

The digestive system contains organs, like the stomach and intestines, that break down the food you eat into proteins, fats, and carbohydrates. Overall, the

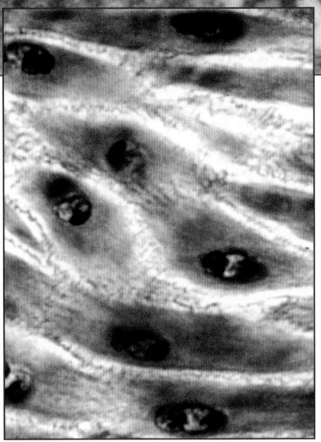

Muscles play a part in the digestive system. Above is a magnified view (x350) of smooth muscle from the stomach wall.

digestive system processes food so it can be absorbed and later used by your body to maintain health and energy. As you will learn in chapter 2, a type of muscle—called smooth muscle—is what powers this process.

The Skeletal System

The skeletal system is made up of bones, ligaments, and tendons. It determines the shape and symmetry of your body, and it acts

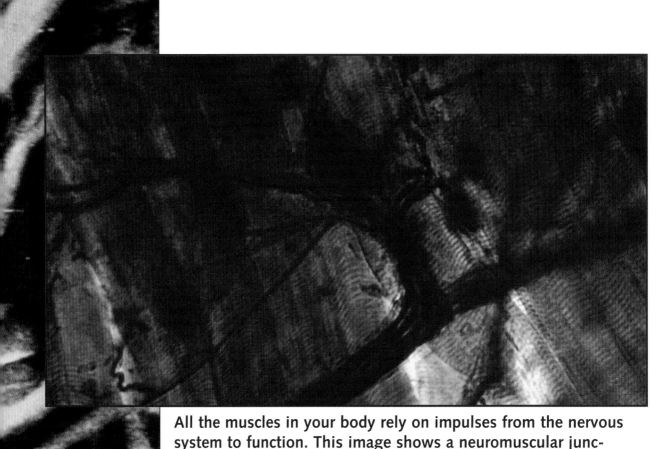

All the muscles in your body rely on impulses from the nervous system to function. This image shows a neuromuscular junction, where nerves connect to muscle tissue.

as a protective shield for your organs. In terms of your muscles, the skeletal system provides a firm base to which muscles can attach. Without your bones, your muscles could not perform the important function of moving your body.

The Nervous System

The nervous system is in charge of sending, receiving, and processing nerve impulses throughout the body. All the organs and muscles inside your body rely on these nerve impulses to function. This is why the nervous system is often referred to as "the master control unit" inside your body.

The Muscular System

You can see that all of the systems within your body are inter dependent, meaning they rely on one another in order for your body to stay in a healthy, properly functioning state. The muscular system functions like this, too. Depending on the movement or function that needs to be performed, different muscles work together for the most efficient outcome. For example, as you will read in chapter 2, something as simple as moving your eyes or tilting your head requires a number of muscles to work together.

Have you ever been so tired that your muscles actually ached from fatigue? Remember how walking up the stairs to your bed seemed like such a long journey, how it felt as though you would never, ever get there? Think about how many times you have woken up late for school and had to run to catch the bus. Human beings depend on their muscles but, as we will discuss in chapter 3, your muscles also depend on you. Taking care of your muscles is incredibly important because your muscles will only do their jobs well if they get what they need: food for energy, rest to recover, and exercise to keep them strong.

If, however, you are taking care of your muscles and you still feel tired or begin to experience aches and pains, something might actually be wrong. In chapter 4 we will talk about some of the problems that you could have with your muscles, like an injury or a disease. We will also discuss different kinds of doctors who specialize in treating people with muscle problems, so you will know who to see if a problem does occur.

The muscular system is fascinating. As you read, try to think of the many different ways that your muscles help you in your life. As you realize how much you need and depend on your muscles, you will begin to see your body in a whole new way.

2

Understanding Your Muscles

There are more than 650 muscles inside the human body. Every moment you are awake and even while you sleep your muscles are in constant motion. When most of us think of muscles, we think about the ones that we use to move our bodies around. In fact, you might lift weights so these muscles become large and defined, or run long distances so your muscles are long and lean. But the muscles you are using when you decide to move are only one type. There are actually three different types of muscle, and two of them you cannot control.

Involuntary Muscles

Your involuntary muscles are those that you cannot consciously control, meaning they will continue to do their jobs whether or not you think about them. For example, you cannot decide to start or stop digesting your food once you have swallowed it. The muscles that line the stomach and the intestines digest and absorb all of the nutrients and vitamins from the food you have just eaten on their own. This is merely one example of some of the human body's involuntary muscles. And, in fact, there are two types of involuntary muscle: smooth muscle and cardiac muscle. Both types perform unique functions inside your body.

Smooth Muscle

Smooth muscle is most involved with the functions of your internal organs. It lines the inside of the stomach, the intestines, and other hollow tubes like the blood vessels. It is also found in the bladder and gallbladder.

Cardiac muscle works involuntarily, continuously pumping blood around the body without tiring.

Cardiac Muscle

Cardiac muscle is made up of the tissue that lines the inside wall of the heart. Unlike other types of muscle, cardiac muscle is not attached to bones or joints, but to other cardiac muscle. It is found only in the heart. The medulla oblongata—a bundle of nerves found at the base of your skull—controls involuntary action throughout your entire body, which includes your cardiac muscle.

Voluntary Muscles

Your voluntary muscles are the muscles that you can control. If you are running up the stairs and you see a toy sitting on the next step, you might decide to skip that step. When you think of skipping the step your brain quickly sends a message to your leg muscle so that it will contract, and raise your leg higher, allowing you to hop over the step and not trip and fall.

Skeletal Muscles

Voluntary muscles make up your skeletal muscle system. This system is composed of all of the muscles that you use to move your body. Overall, skeletal muscle makes up about 40 percent of a man's body and about 23 percent of a woman's.

Skeletal muscle is composed of muscle-cell fibers arranged in groups or bundles. A small muscle may be made of only a few bundles of fibers, while the major muscles in the body can be made up of hundreds of bundles. Each of these muscle fibers has a nerve ending that receives impulses from the brain which stimulates the muscle. When the brain sends neural impulses to certain muscles, those muscles contract and move a specific part of your body.

Major Skeletal Muscles

Skeletal muscle is divided into sections that are defined by where it is located in the body and the function that it performs.

- **Facial**   These are the muscles you use to make facial expressions. The galea aponeurotica, for example, allows you to move your scalp over your skull bone, or cranium. It also helps you raise your eyebrows and wrinkle your forehead.

- **Neck**   The neck area is moved almost entirely by two muscles, called the sternohyoid and the sternocleidomastoid. These muscles work together to move the head left and right, or up and down.

- **Shoulder**   This group of muscles—made up of the trapezius, deltoid, infraspinatus, teres major, and rhomboid major—works together to move the shoulder area. These muscles allow you, for example, to pick up or throw objects.

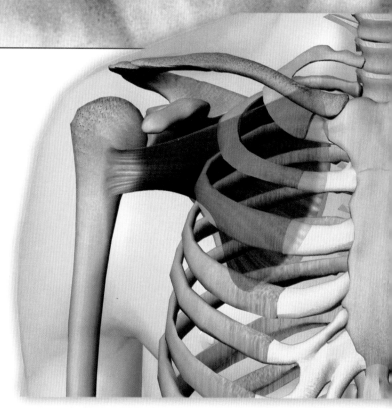

A group of skeletal muscles working together enables you to move your shoulder.

● **Arm** The bicep and tricep are two muscles that you probably know. They are located in the upper part of the arm. The bicep allows you to bring your forearm close to your body, while the tricep allows you to push yourself up off the floor.

● **Forearm** Many of these muscles, like the berachiodialis and palmaris, help control the lower part of the arm and the wrist.

● **Thorax** The thorax—composed of muscles like the pectoralis major and minor, or chest muscles—is the set of muscles that helps support your head, arms, stomach, and many other areas of the upper body. If you do not stretch properly before you a lift a heavy box, these are the muscles that are usually damaged.

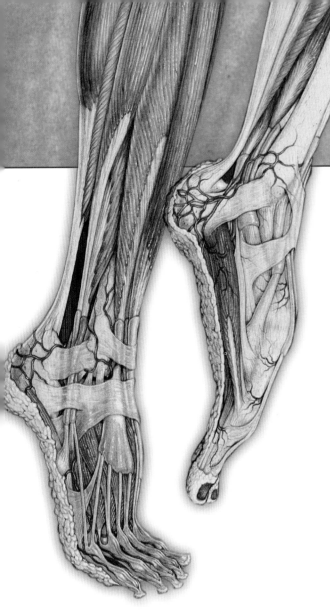

Leg muscles support your body, allow you to move your legs, and absorb impact when you walk or run.

● **Abdomen**   The abdominal area lets you bend down and move your waist from side to side. The internal oblique and external oblique are the two stomach muscles that allow you to move your entire body from left to right.

● **Hip**   This area is made up of the gluteus medius, gluteus maximus, and gluteus minimus—the muscles that make up the buttocks. Their functions range from helping you straighten your leg when you are running, walking, or climbing to lending assistance when you raise your body from a sitting position.

● **Pelvis/Thigh**   This area is made up of muscles like the quadriceps, which occupy the front and side of the thigh, as well as the adductor longus—the long triangular muscle that runs from the pubic bone to the femur or thigh bone. The adductor longus moves the thigh inward and allows it to rotate to the side. These muscles also help you run, walk, and jump.

Leg The leg muscles, including the plantar and dorsal flexors, work together to support your body. They also help you move your leg. For example, a muscle called the tibialis interior, located on the front of the lower leg, helps move the ankle, foot, and toes. The leg muscles also absorb a lot of the impact when you are walking and running.

What Do Muscles Look Like?

All of your muscles are made of fibers that create movement through contraction, or shortening. If you sliced through a muscle you would see that it looks like the inside of a thick wire which is composed of a lot of smaller wires. Like the wire, muscles are composed of groups or bundles of muscle fibers that lay over each other. Also contained in these bundles are your nerves, blood vessels, and connective tissue. Connective tissue plays many roles in the muscular system. For example, a tendon connects muscle to bone, while fascia covers and binds together an entire muscle.

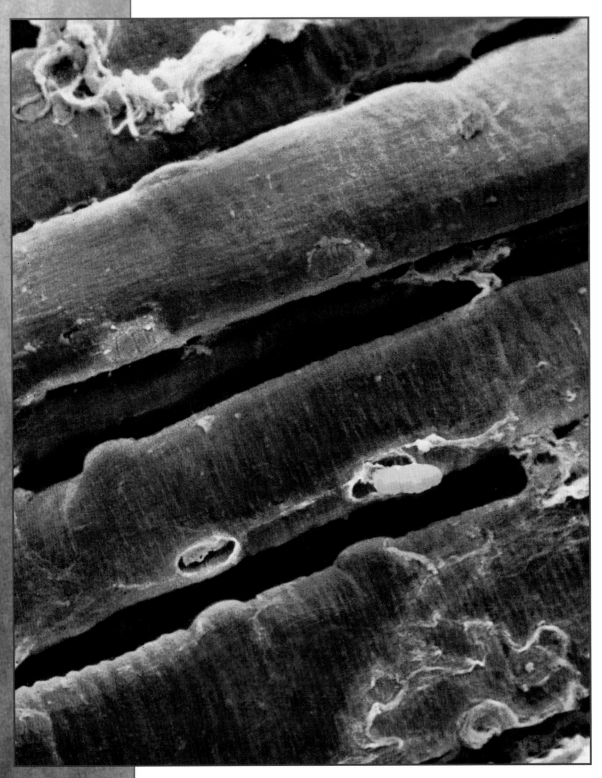

Above is a magnified view (x330) of skeletal muscle fibers. Muscle fibers work together and they are unable to contract unless they all contract at the same time.

How Do Muscles Produce Movement?

Muscles make us capable of so many different actions, but each individual muscle is only really able to perform one task: each muscle can only pull. So how are we able to move?

The body is basically a system of levers—made up of bones and joints—that are moved by your muscles. But if a muscle can only pull, or contract, how can you move your leg in all different directions? The answer is because all muscles work in pairs. One muscle, like the hamstring—which is in the back of your upper leg—pulls the leg back, and the quadriceps muscle—which is on the front of your upper leg—moves the leg forward. Working together in this way, each part of your body can be moved almost any way you wish.

Assistant Movers

You also have muscles called assistant movers that contribute to a specific movement, like when you bend your knee and want your foot to go toward the inside of your thigh. In this action, the hamstring muscle of the thigh is the prime mover, and the sartorious—a muscle that slants across the front of the upper thigh—is the assistant, helping rotate the lower leg toward the inside of your thigh.

Many muscles must work together to perform even the simplest jobs. In fact, even the smallest parts of the muscle, the muscle fibers, must all contract at the same time or none of them can contract. Since muscles work so hard to keep your body in motion, it is important that you do your job and keep your muscles healthy.

3
Healthy Muscles, Healthy Life

It is very important for the health of your muscles, and your body in general, to get out and exercise and to eat a balanced and healthy diet. There are many ways to keep your muscles in great condition, and if your muscles are taken care of, you will be a happier and healthier person.

Nutrition

Since you were a child, you have most likely been told how important it is to maintain a healthy diet. But as a teen, it is even more vital because your body is going through so many changes and growth spurts. So what is the right approach to healthy eating?

The best thing that you can do is eat a variety of foods, as suggested in *Nutrition and Your Health: Dietary Guidelines for Americans*, published by the United States Department of Agriculture and the Department of Health and Human Services. By eating a variety of healthy foods—vegetables, fruits, breads, cereals, rice, pasta, milk, yogurt and cheese, meat, poultry, fish, dried beans and peas, eggs, and nuts—your body will get the many nutrients that it needs.

Aerobic Exercise

Aerobic exercises like running, swimming, and cycling are some of the best ways for you to keep your muscles in shape. The word "aerobic" literally means "with oxygen." Your body constantly requires oxygen. That is why you breathe. The more you move around, the more oxygen your body needs. When you begin to breathe heavily while you are exercising, it is because your body needs more oxygen to keep going.

When you are exercising aerobically, it means that your body is continuing to get the amount of oxygen it needs to keep doing that activity over a long period of time. Any activity that uses large muscle groups, can be maintained continuously for a long period of time, and is rhythmic in nature is a form of aerobic exercise.

MYTH: Fasting (not eating) is a quick way to lose weight.

TRUTH: There are nutrient requirements that must be met, and if you fast for too long, your body will start to shut down. Fasting may result in weight loss, but muscle will be lost as well as fat, and muscle is much harder to develop than fat. The only way to lose weight without hurting yourself is to combine a sensible diet with a proper exercise routine.

Aerobic activity should generally also be low in intensity, meaning you should not be gasping for breath while you are doing it.

How Does Aerobic Activity Help My Body?

Aerobic activity trains the heart, lungs, and cardiovascular system to process and deliver oxygen more efficiently to every part of the body. As the heart muscle becomes stronger, a larger amount of blood can be pumped with each beat. Fewer beats are then required to rapidly carry oxygen to all parts of the body, including the muscles. The muscles are helped by aerobic activity because exercising makes them stronger and increases their blood flow, which keeps them healthy.

Working in Your Target Zone

How do you figure out if you are working at an aerobic level? The medical community has come up with a guide to help people figure out when they are working at a level that is benefiting their health. According to popular guidelines, if your heart is beating at a rate that is 70 to 85 percent of your maximum heart rate, you are benefiting your body the most. This is referred to as your target zone.

To figure out your target zone, you must first know what your maximum heart rate is, which is usually estimated by subtracting your age from 220. To find your target zone, first calculate the heart rates that are 70 and 85 percent of that maximum heart rate. For example, let's say you are thirteen years old. You subtract 13 from 220, giving you 207. Then you take 70 percent of

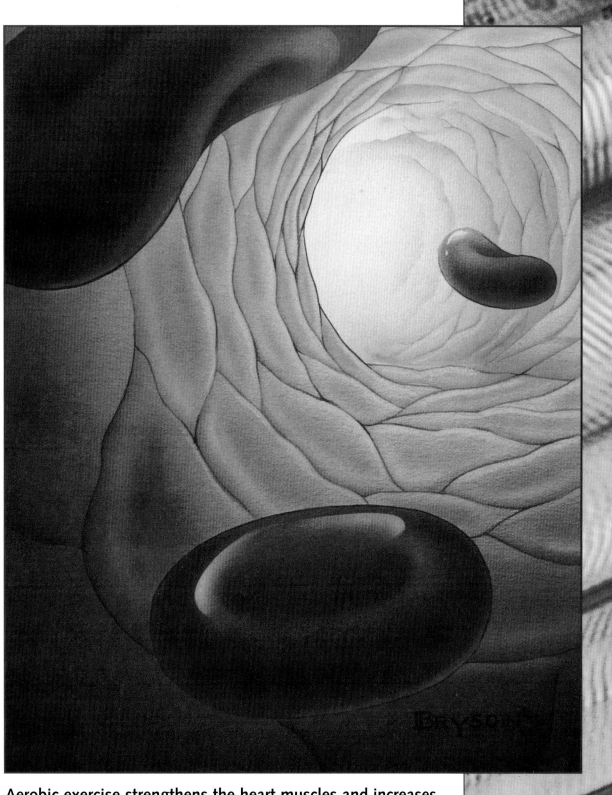

Aerobic exercise strengthens the heart muscles and increases blood flow. This illustration depicts red blood cells floating in an artery.

207 which is 145, and 85 percent of 207 which is 176. By doing this calculation, you find that your target zone is between 145 and 176 beats per minute.

Now that you know your target zone, you can monitor yourself during your workouts by periodically checking your pulse. To do this you can either find your pulse and count the number of times your heart beats in one minute or use a heart rate monitor.

Anaerobic Exercise

What happens if you exercise at a heart rate above your target zone? This is when you move into the anaerobic, "without oxygen," zone. This type of exercise is for those individuals who are already in good physical condition, and should always be supplemented with aerobic activity. You usually know when you are working anaerobically because you will be gasping for breath—your body is not getting the oxygen it needs to maintain that level of activity—and you will not be able to maintain your fast pace for very long. An example of an activity that is anaerobic is sprinting. Anaerobic activities are short bursts of speed or strength.

Strength Training

Strength training activities, like weight lifting, help your muscles stay strong. Strength training is any activity in which you work your muscles against some kind of resistance. Training all areas of your body is the key to maintaining a balanced and well-proportioned body, so you should try to do a combination of weight lifting activities that exercise the muscles in your arms, mid-section, and legs.

Tips for Strength Training

- Begin every workout with five minutes of light aerobic activity and easy stretching.

- Learn proper lifting technique to protect your back and joints from unneeded and unhealthy stress which can quickly lead to injury.

- Use light weights and do many repetitions to avoid injury, especially

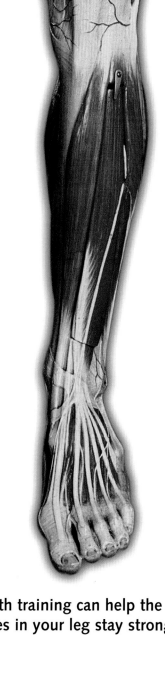

Strength training can help the muscles in your leg stay strong.

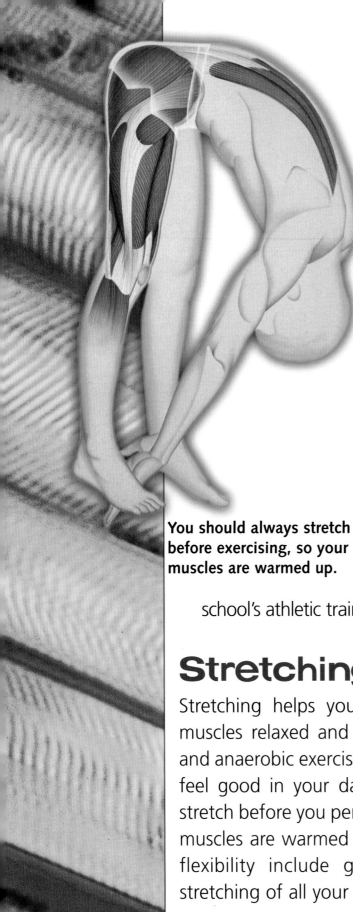

when you are starting your strength training program. (This is very important for teenagers because their bodies are still growing.) If you do wish to increase your weight load, do so gradually and over a long period of time.

● Breathe regularly when doing an exercise.

● Rest for at least one day between your strength training sessions.

● Get advice from your doctor, a coach, or your school's athletic trainer about your exercise program.

You should always stretch before exercising, so your muscles are warmed up.

Stretching

Stretching helps you to move easily, keeping your muscles relaxed and your joints mobile. Like aerobic and anaerobic exercise, regular stretching can help you feel good in your daily life. And you should always stretch before you perform any physical activity so your muscles are warmed up. Activities that heighten your flexibility include gentle reaching, bending, and stretching of all your muscle groups.

Tips for Stretching

● Stretch only to the point where you feel a slight strain in the muscle, not pain

● Stretch slowly and smoothly without bouncing or jerking. Use gentle and continuous movement or stretch and hold for ten to thirty seconds.

● Maintain a steady, natural rhythm of breathing while you stretch.

Muscle is the engine of your body where almost all energy is created by burning fats, carbohydrates, and proteins in the mitochondria, which are the producers of energy inside of each muscle cell. If you exercise, your muscles will stay healthy and burn nutrients efficiently. What this means for you is that, instead of dragging yourself out of bed every morning or coming home from school to take a nap, you will be bursting with motivation during the day, from start to finish.

FUN FACTS

In 490 BC, Pheidippides, a Greek runner, carried the message to Athens that the Persians had invaded the city of Marathon. Back then, even though he died right after reporting the information, he was considered heroic for his ability to run twenty-two miles. This was a remarkable achievement and became the distance of the now-popular marathon race—which has since been extended to twenty-six miles. Some people still do not find this challenging enough, however, and have started running ultra-distance marathons which can be as long as 100 miles.

4

Muscle Injuries, Diseases, and Care

Aches and pains in your muscles are never a good sign. They are your body's way of telling you that something is wrong. In this chapter, symptoms of injury and disease will be talked about, so if you do experience aches and pains in your muscles you will know the difference between a major problem and a minor one. At the end of the chapter, you will also find a brief description of specialists in muscular disorders in case you are having muscle problems.

Common Injuries

Even though you may work hard to keep your muscles healthy, injuries can still happen. You can certainly reduce your chances of getting an injury by being careful, but you can further reduce your risk if you study the best ways to perform exercises. For example, if you decide that you want to be a cyclist or a mountain biker, it is a good idea to learn the proper techniques of rid-

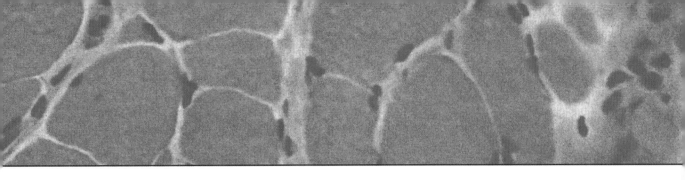

ing. Overuse injuries are more easily avoided if you are knowledgeable about proper form and technique.

Overuse Injuries

Overuse injuries are chronic, meaning that no single event causes them. Instead, they develop slowly from weeks, months, or even years of activity that slowly weakens or irritates the muscles, until exercise eventually becomes difficult or impossible. In many cases, overuse injuries could be avoided if people studied technique, got appropriate rest, and used proper equipment when exercising. Below you will find some of the most common overuse injuries.

Knee Pain

Patellofemoral syndrome refers to generalized knee pain. It is often called runner's knee because it is common among runners. Usually, in the case of runners, the cause is improper running mechanics. For nonrunners, the cause of patellofemoral syndrome is often difficult to pinpoint.

Chondromalacia refers to the wearing away of the cartilage on the back surface of the kneecap; it sounds like your knee is clicking when you move it. Once chondromalacia has occurred, the process is irreversible, so the sufferer basically has to stay away from any activities that cause a lot of pressure on the knees. Overall, it is best to consult a physician or a physical therapist if you feel any sort of pain in your knees.

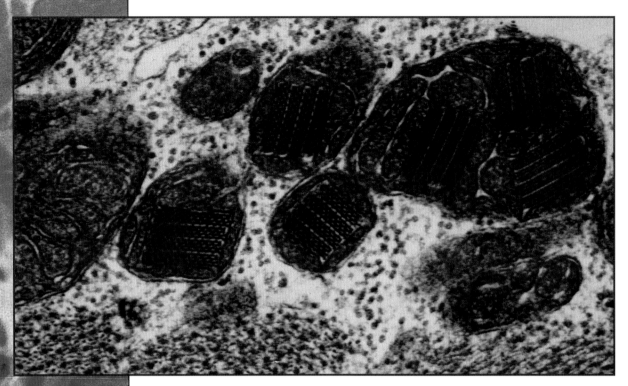

Above is a view of abnormal mitochondria in the muscle of a person with muscle weakness.

Shin Splints and Compartment Syndromes

Shin splints are a common name for pain felt in the front of the calf. Something as minor as muscle imbalances or as serious as a compartment syndrome can cause shin splints. Generally, treatment for shin splints involves strengthening exercises for all of the muscles surrounding the ankle joint, as well as flexibility exercises.

Compartment syndromes are less common than shin splints, but they are also a more serious problem. They occur when the compartments between muscles, which contain blood vessels or nerves, become swollen. This causes the blood vessels to restrict, or grow smaller, leading to pain, swelling, or discomfort.

Tendinitis

Tendinitis most often occurs in athletes because it usually develops from overuse of a tendon or muscle. However, it can also be a result of a direct trauma. The main symptoms of tendinitis are periodic inability to move the affected muscle and sharp, piercing pain.

Diseases of the Muscular System

Some of the diseases that can affect your muscular system cannot be prevented because they are hereditary—you are born with them—or because they are a result of aging. However, no matter what type of disease you may have, living a healthy life can often help lessen the severity of the symptoms.

Muscular Dystrophy

The word "dystrophy" comes from Latin and Greek words that mean "faulty nutrition." When doctors first began studying muscle diseases like muscular dystrophy in the nineteenth century, they didn't have many tools to understand disease other than their own eyes. All they knew about muscular dystrophy was that it caused people's muscles to slowly wear away. Today, we know that muscular dystrophy is caused by the body's inability to create certain proteins that play a role in supporting the structure of muscle fibers. Therefore, the term "muscular dystrophy" actually refers to a group of diseases that weaken and eventually destroy skeletal muscles. Both the smooth and cardiac muscles can also be affected by muscular dystrophy, but this type of the disease is very rare.

Polio

Polio, also known as poliomyelitis, is caused by a virus that attacks the central nervous system. It results in muscle pain and weakness, and in the most severe cases the sufferer becomes paralyzed. In the 1950s, researchers developed a vaccine for polio, so today we are able to prevent people from getting the disease.

Post-Polio Syndrome

There are currently 1.6 million polio survivors within the United States and it is estimated that 50 percent of these people will develop post polio syndrome (PPS). The disease occurs only in people who had polio and happens because the nerves that were damaged during the original illness have never recovered. The most common symptoms of this illness are muscle pain, fatigue, and respiratory and sleeping problems.

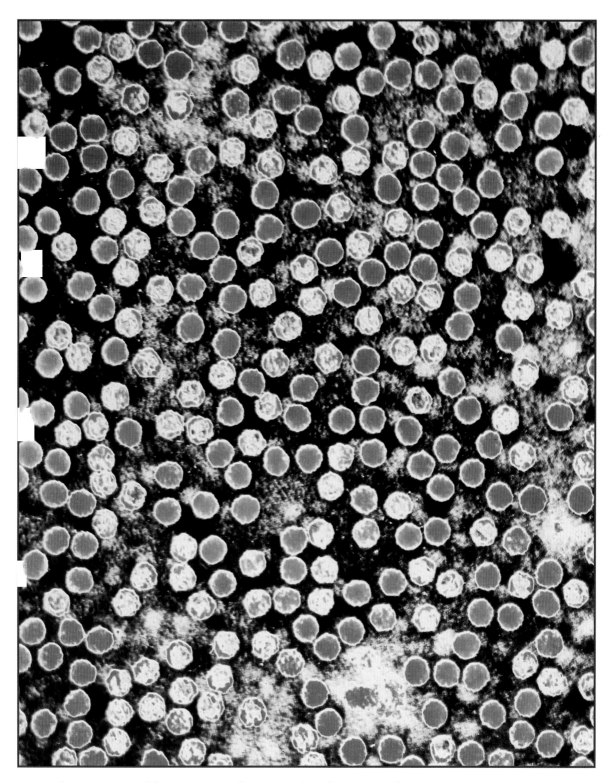

Polio is caused by a virus that attacks the central nervous system. This image (magnification x64,000) shows numerous poliovirus particles.

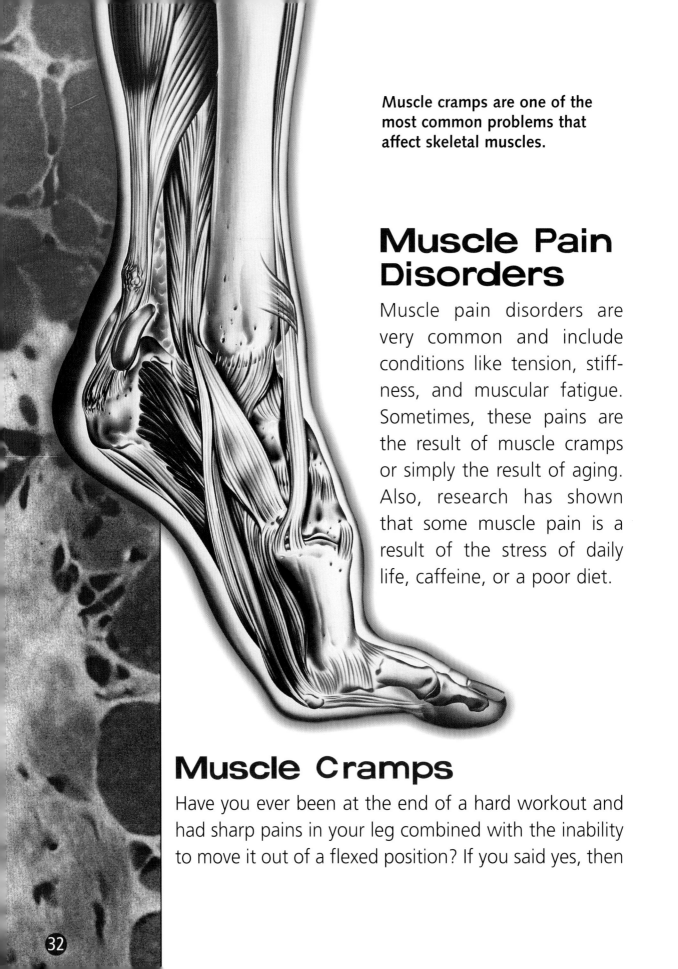

Muscle cramps are one of the most common problems that affect skeletal muscles.

Muscle Pain Disorders

Muscle pain disorders are very common and include conditions like tension, stiffness, and muscular fatigue. Sometimes, these pains are the result of muscle cramps or simply the result of aging. Also, research has shown that some muscle pain is a result of the stress of daily life, caffeine, or a poor diet.

Muscle Cramps

Have you ever been at the end of a hard workout and had sharp pains in your leg combined with the inability to move it out of a flexed position? If you said yes, then it is most probably a muscle cramp that you experienced, one of the most common problems that affect muscles.

Skeletal muscle cramps during exercise happen when a muscle that is shortened is repeatedly stimulated, or used for a long period of time. The muscle gets fatigued and doesn't relax properly between contractions. Instead, the reflex arc—nerves in charge of carrying signals from the muscle to the central nervous system and then back again—keeps carrying signals to the muscle that tell it to stay contracted, which causes a cramp. Another reason for cramps is a low amount of electrolytes like potassium and calcium in the body. Cold weather can also cause your muscles to cramp.

Aging

Aging is unavoidable and does take its toll on your muscles. As muscles get older, they lose their ability to perform at their best. Muscle size and strength often diminish, causing older people to be more frail and less agile. They cannot move as quickly or with the ease and grace they had when they were younger.

People Who Take Care of Your Muscles

We have talked about how taking care of your muscles is an especially important goal. But sometimes injuries do occur. When this happens, it is important to treat the injury and return the muscle to full working capacity. Below are some of the doctors and trained professionals you can work with if you are injured or experiencing general aches and pains. A few of them can also be contacted if you just want to ask some questions about your exercise habits to make sure you stay injury-free.

Athletic Trainer

An athletic trainer provides aid to injured athletes. Whether an athlete has a muscle cramp or is recovering from time spent in a cast, an athletic trainer is concerned with keeping athletes in their healthiest shape or returning them to health as quickly as possible. Some of an athletic trainer's main goals are to educate athletes on the many ways they can prevent injuries when exercising and to guide an injured athlete through the process of rehabilitation—a process that will hopefully allow an athlete to make a full recovery.

Physical Therapist

Much like an athletic trainer, a physical therapist, or PT, is a trained health professional who treats people with health problems resulting from injuries, but also helps people who are suffering from disease. A physical therapist looks at joint motion, muscle strength and endurance, durability of the heart and lungs, and how well the injured person can perform daily life activities. Some of the treatments he or she might suggest include therapeutic exercise, cardiovascular endurance training, and training in activities of daily living.

Massage Therapist

More and more people are becoming patients of massage therapists because they want relief from injuries or because they believe massage will help them deal with the stresses of daily life. A massage can help relieve tension, or "knots" in your muscles, increase circulation through

A massage can relieve tension and increase circulation through your muscles.

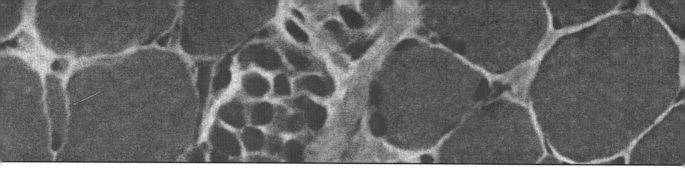

your muscles, and, if done on a regular basis, can improve your overall health. Getting a rubdown from a trained professional can also help an athlete recover from tough training and decreases chances of injury. At this time, most doctors will not recommend that you see a massage therapist, but if you ask them for their opinion most will agree that massages are beneficial to your health.

Cardiologist

A cardiologist is the kind of doctor you would see if you were having problems with your heart. Remember that cardiac muscle is only found in the heart, so these doctors specialize in this type of muscle tissue, as well as the overall organ. You might see a cardiologist if you are experiencing a rapid heartbeat or palpitations—an irregular heartbeat that feels like a slight fluttering in your chest. Because the heart is such a complex organ, depending on what problem you are diagnosed with, treatment can range from taking better care of your heart by exercising daily to surgery.

Kinesiologist

Kinesiology is the science of studying body movement. A kinesiologist's job is to increase the activity level and total well-being of the person he or she is treating. There are many different fields within kinesiology; a practitioner may concentrate on the respiratory system or work to resolve problems with a patient's movement. A kinesiologist who focuses on rehabilitation would perform muscle testing

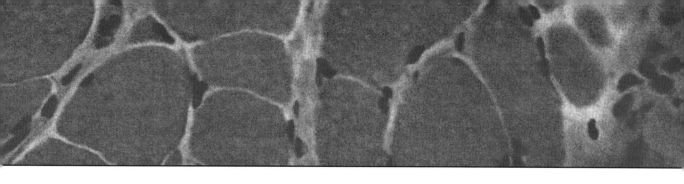

to evaluate any structural, mental, or nutritional problems that you may have. An occupational kinesiologist often works for a company and deals with issues like employee fitness and the design of equipment that employees must use every day. If you have to see a kinesiologist, you should expect to be evaluated just like you would be by your family doctor. However, a kinesiologist will be looking for movement problems. If he or she finds one, the next step would be to create a rehabilitation program for you.

Your Muscles: A Final Word

The muscular system is very intricate. It allows you to move through your life with ease and makes sure your body continues functioning. As you now know, the relationship between your muscles and feeling good cannot be ignored. Good nutrition and regular exercise are two ways that you can keep your muscles in good shape. Remember, the more fit you are, the less chance there is that you will ever have to deal with the diseases and injuries that we have discussed. And now that you know all about your muscles, stretch out and relax!

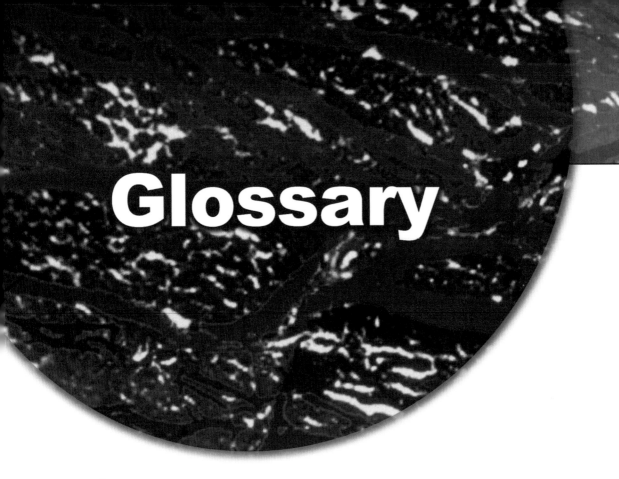

Glossary

assistant movers
Muscles that help to make a specific movement, like when you bend your knee and rotate it inward.

blood vessels
Made up of the veins and arteries, these tubelike structures carry blood through your body.

capillaries
One-cell-thick blood vessels that run from the muscular fibers to the arteries and veins.

cardiac muscle
Muscle tissue that is found only in the heart.

compartment syndrome
Problem that occurs when compartments between muscles become swollen, leading to pain, swelling, and discomfort.

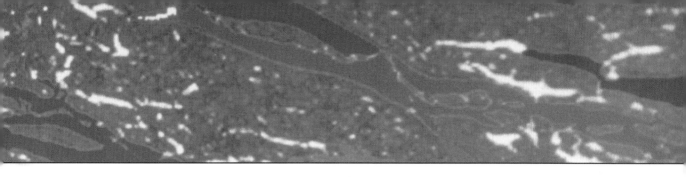

maximum heart rate
The base figure that is used to determine your target heart rate; figured out by subtracting your age from 220.

muscle fibers
Small fibers found within the muscles that hold nerves, blood vessels, and connective tissue.

muscular dystrophy
A group of diseases that destroy the skeletal muscles; caused by the body not being able to create certain proteins.

shin splints
A common athletic injury that causes pain in the front of the calf.

skeletal muscle
Muscle tissue in the body that powers movement of the skeleton.

smooth muscle
Forms the supporting tissue of blood vessels and hollow internal organs such as the stomach, intestines, and gall bladder.

target heart rate (or target zone)
Rate at which your heart should beat during aerobic exercise; should be between 70 and 85 percent of your maximum heart rate.

For More Information

In the United States

American Council on Science and Health
1995 Broadway
Second Floor
New York, NY 10023-5860
(212) 362-7044
Web site: http://www.acsh.org

Center for Food Safety and Applied Nutrition
200 C Street SW
Washington, DC 20204
Web site: http://www.cfsan.fda.gov

Health Central
6001 Shellmound Street, Suite 800
Emeryville, CA 94608

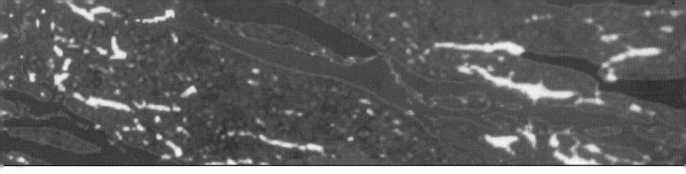

(510) 250-2500
e-mail: communications@healthcentral.com
Web site: http://www.healthcentral.com

Muscular Dystrophy Association
National Headquarters
3300 E. Sunrise Drive
Tucson, AZ 85718
(800) 572-1717
e-mail: mda@mdausa.org
Web site: http://www.mdausa.org

Shape Up America
6707 Democracy Boulevard, Suite 306
Bethesda, MD 20817
e-mail: suainfor@shapeup.org
Web site: http://www.shapeup.org

Youth and Children Net
Streetcats Foundation
267 Lester Avenue, Suite 104
Oakland, CA 94606
e-mail: youthkids@aol.com
Web site: http://www.enn2.com/teencity.htm

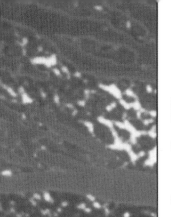

In Canada

Canadian Society for Exercise Physiology
185 Somerset Street West, Suite 202
Ottawa, ON K2P 0J2
(877) 651-3755
e-mail: info@csep.ca
Web site: http://www.csep.ca

Health Canada
Tunney's Pasture PL 1910A1
Ottawa, ON K1A 1B4
(416) 913-4389
e-mail: hpo@hc-sc.qc.ca
Web site: http://www.hc-sc.gc.ca

Health Support Link
KJR NetLinks
151 Tansley Drive
Carp, ON K0A 1L0
(613) 831-8773
Web site: http://www.healthsupportlink.com

Science World British Columbia
1455 Quebec Street
Vancouver, BC V6A 3Z7
(604) 443-7443
e-mail: neng@scienceworld.bc.ca
Web site: http://www.scienceworld.bc.ca

Web Sites

AMA Health Insight
http://www.ama-assn.org

BodyQuest
http://library.thinkquest.org/10348/

Fitness Online
http://www.fitnessonline.com

FitTeen
http://www.fitteen.com

Galaxy of Health
http://www.galaxyofhealth.com

How Stuff Works
http://www.howstuffworks.com/sports-physiology.htm

For Further Reading

Avila, Victoria. *How Our Muscles Work*. Broomall, PA: Chelsea House Publishers, 1995.

Feinberg, Brian, Dale C. Garell (ed.), and Solomon H. Snyder (ed.). *The Musculoskeletal System*. Broomall, PA: Chelsea House Publishers, 1994.

Figtree, Dale. *Eat Smart: A Guide to Good Health for Kids*. Clinton, NJ: New Win Publishing, 1997.

Galperin, Anne. *Nutrition*. Broomall, PA: Chelsea House Publishers, 1991.

Ganeri, Anita. *Moving*. Chatham, NJ: Raintree/Steck-Vaughn Publishers, 1994.

Parker, Steve. *The Human Body*. Alexandria, VA: Time-Life, Inc., 1997.
————. *Muscles*. Brookfield, CT: Copper Beech Books, 1997.

Savage, Jeff. *Fundamental Strength Training*. Minneapolis, MN: The Lerner Publishing Group, 1998.

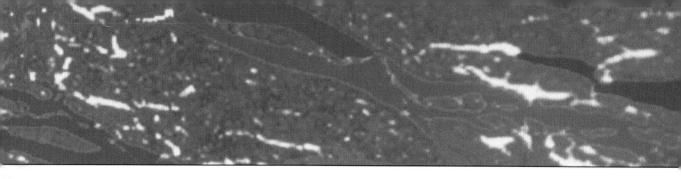

Silverstein, Alvin, Robert Silverstein, and Virginia B. Silverstein. *The Muscular System.* New York: Twenty-First Century Books, Inc., 1995.

West, Dorothy F. *Nutrition and Fitness: Lifestyle Choices for Wellness*. Tinley Park, IL: Goodheart-Wilcox, 1999.

White, Lee, Caesar Pacifici, and Mary Ditson. *The Teenage Human Body Operator's Manual*. Eugene, OR: Northwest Media, Inc., 1998.

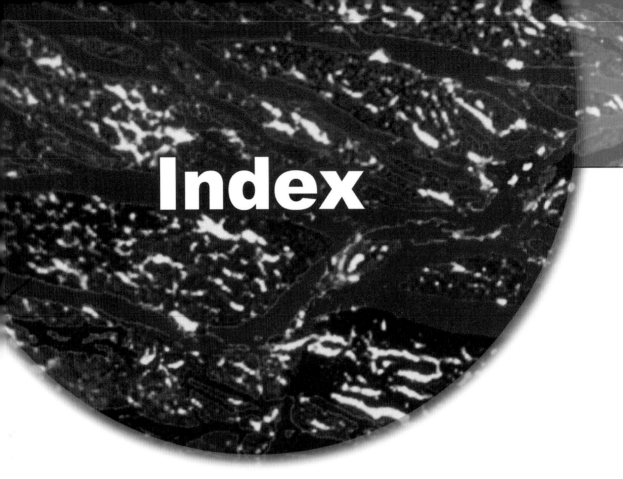

Index

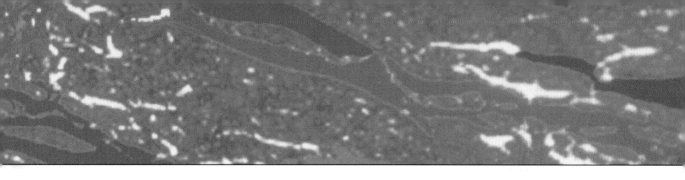

Credits

About the Author
Katherine White is a writer and editor who lives in Brooklyn, New York.

Photo Credits
P. 5 © Biophoto Associates/Photo Researchers, Inc.; p. 6 © Lester V. Bergman/Corbis; p. 10 © Quest/Science Photo Library; p. 13 © Life ART; p. 14 © Professor Peter Cull/Science Photo Library; p. 16 © Professors P.M. Motta, P.M. Andrews, K.R. Porter and J.Vial/Science Photo Library; p. 21 © 1997 Bryson Biomedical Illustrations; p. 23 © Biophoto Associates; p. 24 © 1995 Leonard D. Dank; p. 28 © Biophoto Associates; p. 31 © A.B. Dowsett/Science Photo Library; pp. 32, 35 © John Bavosi/Science Photo Library.
Cover, front matter, and back matter © Custom Medical Stock Photo and © John Daugherty/Photo Researchers, Inc.: tissue section of cardiac muscle and illustration of muscles of adult male .
Ch. 1 © 1992 Robert Becker, Ph.D.: electron micrograph of muscle, showing banding.
Ch. 2 © John Daugherty/Photo Researchers, Inc.: illustration of chest muscles of adult human (extreme close-up).
Ch. 3 © Michael Abbey/Science Source: human striated muscle (magnification x106).
Ch. 4 © Biophoto Associates/Science Source: smooth muscle from the stomach wall (magnification x350).

Series Design
Cindy Williamson

Layout Design
Danielle Goldblatt